IMAGINATION
A MYSTICAL TECHNOLOGY

DR. JIMMIE REED

Title: Imagination: A Mystical Technology
By: Dr. Jimmie Reed
Cover Design: Tracy Fagan
Cover Photograph: agsandrew/Shutterstock.com
Copyright © 2022 Dr. Jimmie Reed

All rights reserved. Printed in the United States of America. No part of this publication may be reproduced in any form without written permission from www.Kingdom-Publishing.com

Kingdom Publishing
PO Box 630443
Highlands Ranch, CO 80163
All rights reserved.

Scripture quotations taken from the Amplified® Bible (AMP), Copyright © 2015 by The Lockman Foundation. Used by permission. www.lockman.org

ISBN 978-1-737515685 (print)
ISBN 978-1-737515692 (ebook)

Table of Contents

Introduction............................ 5

Potential............................... 9

Revelation 13

Frequency............................. 15

Living in Mediocrity 17

Imagination 21

Now It's Your Turn................... 29

Recommended Resources 33

About the Author..................... 35

Connect with Dr. Reed 39

Introduction

The desire to move forward and experience new things is programmed inside each one of us. You can see a glimpse of this when you watch children at play. Give them a couple of blankets and some chairs and they make a rocket ship, become astronauts, and are soon on their way to the moon.

What if you could rekindle your *imagination* by taking a fresh look at ways utilize your mind to move forward? Incorporating all of your senses will bring your dreams and visions not just into focus, but manifest them into reality!

I have found, by engaging my *imagination*, I have fostered my ambition and been catapulted into action. It has kept me from wandering in circles because there is always another way to navigate the situation. By posing the question, "What else is possible?" or "How can this be different?" is a quick way to move from the place called "stuck."

> Imagination is a technology built into our DNA.

Where do the innovative ideas come from when you are called on to be creative? Whether it's solving problems, painting a landscape, or designing a new building, your *imagination* is the source for these great ideas! Through the *imagination* we have the capacity to begin to see images or concepts of what is currently not present to our senses.

Imagination is a technology built into our DNA. Technology is the application of knowledge for practical purposes. When we allow our *imagination* to solve problems and create new possibilities, we are drawing from deep inside to find a solution. It is something we can innately do; which means it is built into our DNA.

Imagination is the faculty of imaging, or of forming mental images or concepts of what is not actually present to the senses.

Synonyms: ingenuity, enterprise, thought

Many years ago, I imagined being able to hear clearly from God and speaking to others about what I was hearing and seeing. As I began to do that, I was seeing people relieved of pain and sickness. I could sense a shift beyond the natural healing, but a change in the spiritual realm as well.

Every day, I imagine becoming more excellent in every aspect of my targeted pursuit. As long as I envision this, my pursuit will bring me to a place of becoming who I am, what I was created for, and why I was released into the earth realm.

> "Logic can take you from A to B.
> Imagination *can take you everywhere.*"
> ~Albert Einstein

It all starts in our mind. That which we think about will eventually be spoken. When we speak, the words we say begin to create around us. We begin to draw into our space what we are seeing. We create!

> *"Imagination is everything. It's the preview to life's coming attractions."*
> ~Albert Einstein

POTENTIAL

You were born with great potential. All men are sent to the world with limitless credit, a reservoir of great ideas and abilities; but seldom draw to their full extent.

Potential is dormant ability, reserved power, untapped strength, unused success, hidden talents, and capped capability.
- Myles Munroe

Think of it as what you can be, but have not yet become; all you can do, but have not done. All you can reach, but have not yet reached. What you can accomplish, but have not yet accomplished. Potential is unexposed ability and latent power.

In other words, what you have already done is no longer your potential. So, unless you do something beyond what you have done, you will never grow or experience your full potential.

Everything in life is created from potential.

Imagination can keep you from being satisfied with your last accomplishment.

We are responsible for the potential stored within us. We must learn to understand it and effectively use it. Too often, a measure of success prevents us from delving deeper into that which lies within us. In that case, success makes us complacent and becomes our enemy. *Imagination* can keep you from being satisfied with your last accomplishment.

Every seed has the potential to become a plant. Every bird has the potential to become part of a flock. Every cow can join others to become a herd.

When potential is unrealized, visions die unseen, songs die unsung, plans die unexecuted, and bright futures lie buried in the past.

We must not be distracted by the appearance that something is impossible. Nor can we let what we cannot do interfere with what we can do. In the early 1950's the world believed it was impossible to run a mile in under four minutes. May 6, 1954, British athlete Roger Bannister crossed the finish line of the one-mile race at 3:59.4 – doing "the impossible." Once Bannister showed the impossible to be possible, that record for the fastest mile has been broken eighteen times, and now sits at 3:43.13, held by Hicham El Guerrouj of Morocco.

Let go of what you thought was impossible. With the help of God, all things are possible.

Focusing on and doing what you can do will keep you moving towards your imagined goal. Executing new actions expands your mind to the potential inside of you.

Principles to Help Understand Your Potential

It is imperative to get the revelation that God is the source of all potential. He spoke the universe and everything in it into being. In other words, everything that was invisible became visible. God saw. (Genesis 1)

Everything in life has potential.

It is imperative to get the revelation God is the source of all potential. In the beginning the earth was all water. He spoke to the universe and everything in it into existence. He saw possibilities and caused change. In other words, what He saw became tangible. There are endless possibilities, but oftentimes we don't see them. Once we allow our *imagination* to become a participator, we have a vision of what could be. Then we are able to set goals to accomplish what we see.

Nothing in life is instant.

We can ask the question, "When did Albert Einstein become a genius?" Was it when he received the Nobel Peace prize in 1921? Maybe it was when he discovered the formula $E=mc^2$. Maybe he was a genius when he was born; and the process of releasing his potential over time is what revealed who God created him to be.

Never settle for what you have.

Potential is always present, waiting to manifest. It demands we never settle for what we have already accomplished. Our present state in life isn't final. It is just the time between what has been done and the potential of what can happen.

Success comes from seeing potential in a new way.

If we are to be effective in this season, we need to see our potential in a way we have not seen before. God is releasing fresh revelation. The seer anointing, or God showing people through visions and dreams, is being released in a greater way. We need to open our spiritual eyes to see what God is showing us.

Let's look at the potential God placed in Abram. The Lord said to Abram, "Leave your country, your people and your father's household and go to the land I will show you." (Genesis 12:2) God began revealing to Abram, whose name was later changed to Abraham, the potential that was inside of him. It wasn't an instant process. Abram had to leave his familiar surroundings, and follow God. As the story continues on, God revealed the potential inside Abraham, which included being the father of many nations. But if he never took the first action, the rest of the process wouldn't have taken place.

Revelation

How do you begin to understand the potential that has been placed inside you? That is a great question! That is why we ask God for revelation, to make known something that was previously secret or unknown.

Revelation is a divine or supernatural disclosure to humans of a surprising and previously unknown fact, especially one that is made known in a dramatic way.

There are seasons that require fresh revelation in order to have a clear-cut goal. The Greek word for revelation is apocalypses and means "an uncovering or disclosure." New Webster's dictionary defines reveal as to make known, manifest, to reveal one's real intention. It defines revelation as "the manifestations of God Himself to man." Simply put, revelation is God disclosing Himself and all of His wisdom to us.

Getting that first glimpse of what we are to do, or what we are called to be is like having a seed impregnated in us; then *imagination* keeps it alive and active. When this seed is fostered and fueled, we watch the growth of that very thing all the way from inception to birth to full expression. Therefore; seek, believe, and act on revelation.

In the biblical sense, revelation is simply God revealing Himself or His will. It is to bring forth or disclose something that has been hidden or unknown. If we spend time in God's presence, He will unveil insights and truth that will cause us to see our breakthrough.

Frequency

With greater understanding about our potential and revelation knowledge; let's look at how we begin activating our *imagination*. The more you exercise this great mystical technology you've been given…the greater the strength you carry to achieve and receive what it is you have imagined.

If we look at the example of God creating everything from nothing, He spoke things into existence. There is power in the frequency of your words.

Dr. Masaru Emoto, founder of the International Health Medical Company, is known for his scientific findings that demonstrate and help us to understand how words and frequency impact organic things around us. For example, he conducted an experiment with rice. The same amount of rice was placed into three separate containers and sealed. One container was spoken to with harsh hatred filled words while the second container of rice was ignored. The third was spoken to in very loving words. The rice the container that received harsh words began to turn a greenish color, while the rice that was ignored turned black. The rice that had loving words spoken to it was mostly white a with slight yellowing after a couple of months.

We could see a physical manifestation from the words spoken to the rice. Our *imagination* and potential react in a similar way to the thoughts and words we hold towards it. It is important to speak life over your inventive ideas and creative solutions.

When you speak, the frequency of your words begins to create. Those words are the seeds planted; and they begin to grow and develop into what you are seeing.

When you open your mouth, and describe your *imagination* through words, you have won half the battle. The frequency of the words latches on to the preceding thoughts and continues to press the idea forward. With prayer and continued revelation, you are well on your way to exploring many new things.

In the experiment mentioned above, the words were actually spoken. However, unspoken words produce a frequency released through our thoughts. This is one of the reasons we are encouraged to keep our minds focused on that which is pure, trustworthy, excellent, of good report, and praiseworthy. (Philippians 4:8) To further strengthen the connection between thoughts and spoken words, we are told in the Bible, that which you think about will eventually be spoken out through your mouth. (Matthew 15:18)

What we think brings outcome of the very thing we are thinking about or imagining. So, as you work to embrace your *imagination*, it is important to align your thoughts with your words – and make sure they both are supportive to fulfilling your potential.

Living in Mediocrity

Mediocrity is the state of being moderate or of low quality, value, ability. There is no reason for a single one of us to be living a ho-hum life. As humans, we are created in the image of God, the creator of the Universe. (Genesis 1:27)

So why do so many people live a life of just getting by? It is because they have no vision and have ignored and quieted their *imagination*, their dreaming, and their believing!

Let's look at some characteristics of a mediocre life. Take note if you can relate to any of these.

Compromise

The word compromise, when used as a verb, is defined as "to make a shameful or disreputable concession." Compromise happens when you water down your dreams or settle for less; it takes you away from living your best life. If something you try doesn't end the way you expected, that isn't compromise. Compromise comes when you choose to give up and accept those results as enough. Remember every step you take on your pathway in life is designed to move you to another place.

Living an uncompromising life is not easy. There are times when we have to push and press pass difficult situations. We must fight to conquer giants. The minute we start to compromise, or settle for less, that is we go backward.

Indecision

An average life is characterized by indecision; a wavering between two or more possible courses of action. It's important to realize that indecision is a decision; the decision to do nothing. When you do nothing, nothing changes; and when nothing changes, mediocracy moves in.

We all experience the proverbial fork in the road; but to move forward, you must ask God for wisdom, gather information, listen to your spirit… and then DO SOMETHING!!! You can always change course, but you will never experience the great life you were designed to have if you sit in indecision.

Wrong Thinking

What is your mind telling you about yourself and your life? If it is saying you're an average joe, and it isn't going to get any better than this, your mind it's lying to you. You are above average; and there is so much more you can do. A life of mediocracy is infused with thoughts that you aren't good enough, you don't know enough, or you failed last time so there is no use in trying again.

Abundant living starts in your thinking, because as we discussed before, whatever is in your thoughts will eventually come out in your words; and words have the frequency to create the world around you.

Lack of Vision, or Sight for Your Future

If you don't know where you are headed, you are headed nowhere. The schedule of an average life consists of getting up, doing what you did yesterday, eating, watch someone else's dreams, AKA the television, going to bed, and repeating.

Vision is defined as an ideal or goal toward which one aspires. God does not want us to remain stuck in a place of mediocrity. Let your *imagination* kick in when slothfulness or mediocrity tries to discourage you on the path headed towards your vision. If you don't have a vision, use your *imagination* to create one! We must defeat the enemy called average.

Lack of Counsel

When you see a mediocre life in action, one thing that will be missing is wise counsel. We need others in our lives to encourage us during our personal journey, help us to see things from a different perspective, and give sober advice. God tells us, without counsel, purposes and plans fail. (Proverbs 15:22)

Move towards an amazing life and find others who are doing the same. Instead of talking about people and things, talk about ideas and dreams! Seeking out input of others keep us from falling into mediocrity and settling for 'average.'

IMAGINATION

Now that we have an understanding of the power of our thoughts and words; and know how to recognize an average or mediocre life, let's look at how we can use our *imagination* to experience an extraordinary life. *Imagination* helps you to overcome the enemy called average, we must conquer these hindrances and mindsets.

Simply put, *imagination* is a door, a gateway, or a foreseen idea being challenged to become reality. Once you step into that door or gateway, it is no longer *imagination*, or just an idea because you step into it. You have started to manifest something out of nothing.

So where do you get the courage to step into the door your *imagination* has created? Faith. The Greek word for faith is pistis. The Strong's Concordance defines faith as "the conviction of truth of anything, belief." Once we begin to think about and see things in our mind that haven't manifested as of yet, we need to bolster our faith, to believe they can manifest into the natural world.

Unfortunately, our westernized attitude scoffs, mocks, and de-values the mechanism of *imagination*. Many will chastise this as day-dreaming as wasting time and energy on something that isn't real or worthwhile. This is how many of us have been taught to stop imagining.

Trauma is another hinderance of *imagination*. When someone

has experienced trauma and hasn't worked to resolve the mental and emotional impact, the thoughts, feelings, and beliefs tied to that trauma continue to play in their mind, either consciously or subconsciously. Statistics show that someone who was abused in their childhood is more likely to marry an abuser. They think the thoughts of never marrying an abuser. However, the thoughts of the abuse playing over in their mind, releases a frequency and becomes a drawing factor.

Experiencing Different Realms

The concept of *imagination* is so powerful is because there are other realms connected to the earthly realm we physically live in and see. When we begin to think about all the possibilities, we must take into consideration the entire universe. Because both exist, we are a part of one another. We both carry power that connect and create.

Imagination takes us into another realm because we have ventured out into an unseen territory that, until you step in, it is unreachable. Recognizing you are seated in higher places than in the earth, we begin to draw from that which is not seen.

There are two realms, the mystical, or thought realm and the natural realm. The thought realm is in your mind, and the natural real is one you experience through your senses. Both are real.

Imagination comes through the unseen, or mystical realm and brings ideas to be created in the natural realm. After all, someone imagined every style of chair you've ever sat in, every model of a car you've ever driven, and every type of house or apartment you have ever lived in. Everything you see came from someone's *imagination*.

Mystical means of or relating to direct communication with God or absolute truth.

IMAGINATION: A MYSTICAL TECHNOLOGY

A mystic is one who believes in unseen realities. One who believes they can have access to hidden mysteries, transcending ordinary human knowledge. One who believes they can actually know God.

As you explore your *imagination*, you are moving into the unseen realm, and transcending ordinary human knowledge. You are seeking God to learn of things He has created but have not yet been seen. As you explore, you will receive ideas, visions, and dreams.

Dr. Paul Yongii Cho, pastor of one of the world's largest Protestant churches in Seoul, South Korea, suggests visions and dreams are the language of a fourth dimension.

In his book titled *The Fourth Dimension: Discovering a New World of Answered Prayer*, Dr. Cho describes the fourth dimension is a spiritual sphere. It's the realm where our human spirits, our faith, belief, and *imagination* can link up with God to create, and manifest here in the third dimension.

It is important to mention that the fourth dimension is also used by the devil. In this spiritual sphere, human spirit can link up with evil spirits and counterfeits. Therefore, in this new season, we must be careful and diligent to join our spirits with the fourth dimension of the Holy Spirit, that we may fulfill the vision we have been given to dominate in the earth.

The way you connect with Holy Spirit versus evil is through intention and frequency. Frequency is energy that can be created by our *imagination* as a vehicle to open portals and doors into the other realm. When you set a certain frequency around you, it will attract either good or evil. I personally desire to live in two realms at the same time by attracting angels and other angelic beings.

Don't Tell Your Big Dreams to Small Minded People

A great way to begin to engage your *imagination* is by dreaming. As you dream, it is important you guard what your *imagination* is telling you from those who will kill it. This includes yourself. We can kill our own dreams with negativity about it. Do not say words that can sabotage you. Make sure to keep the vision of what you are called to pursue. You must realize that our words carry a frequency, that once in the atmosphere, sets itself on a forever journey. The words you speak and the thoughts you think will start a frequency that attaches to the entire universe, and because you have been made with great power, these words will make sure it will reach its destiny of that which was spoken. Use your *imagination* to produce positive energy that will cause a much better outcome.

I was a personal trainer, helping others to eat healthy and exercise. In my *imagination*, I saw a portable flexible floor that I could use to various exercises such as jogging, jumping jacks, and muscle toning. It would be portable, so I could lift it and store it behind a door; setting it up for everyday workouts. It was something I had never seen in any store before. I shared my idea with someone in my home and was told, "I can't see that." It was discouraging for a moment. That statement sought to dampen my *imagination*. I went on to further explain the concept, but because they could not see it, they offered no help. I bypassed what I had been told by that individual and began to build it myself. I created the aerobic board. I was building and selling them for several years until we received orders to move overseas. This flexible board helped me to maintain a healthy weight when I couldn't go outside in the heat of the summer, the cold of winter, or on rainy days.

This is just one of many things that were in my *imagination* that have come to pass. However; as you can see in this experience, I could have been stopped or greatly delayed by sharing my vision with a small minded individual, or listening to negative feedback.

The person who couldn't see my idea happened to be very important in my life. If that person would have backed me…who knows…perhaps I could have patented and marketed this item, moving forward to help others.

It isn't just others who can sabotage the gifts of your *imagination*. As I mentioned, you can do it to yourself. If you have a vision that is different from what the world knows, don't talk yourself out of chasing it. Use your *imagination* to produce positive energy and find the path to creating that vision.

Be encouraged! You have a destiny to be pursued. No matter how challenging things may look now, there is always something greater. As you keep moving forward remember you are significant. God said He has more for you than you could ever ask or think. (Ephesians 3:20) Join God in His thoughts for you. Allow your *imagination* to take you into the destiny God has planned for you.

The Bigger Picture

There is a purpose for you as you travel your life's road. *Imagination* helps us push through, because things aren't always what they seem to be. In other words what you may be going through at any time, does not mean you will be going through it six months or even a year from now. You can move through to a better place because you have been given a brilliant tool that can be used any time you desire…your *imagination*.

One reason it's important for each of us to use our *imagination* is because your life isn't about you. You were created and called to affect the earth and the others around you. Your *imagination* holds the keys, not just for you but to impact others as well. The things you *imagine* and act upon, for example the paths you take or the inventions you create, are designed to touch and impact other people's lives. Think of the Wright brothers. They died decades ago, but the result of their *imagination*, the airplane, had forever changed our world.

Our *imagination* can guide us to the path God has created for us in our lives. A friend of mine told me he knew he wanted to be a firefighter from a young age. When he was in elementary school, they had firemen come into the classroom to talk about their job. They shared stories of how they rescue people, put out fires, and help the community. This presentation sparked my friend's *imagination*. He is now in his fifteenth year as a firefighter, and receiving continual promotions. He loves his work, and has never regretted his choice. His *imagination* placed him in is destiny; and has helped many people because of it.

So, *dream and imagine BIG* not small. Be willing to take the risk. There is risk in anything worthwhile, so don't be afraid to *imagine* outside of the box. You never know how your contribution to the world is designed to impact others.

Goals

Without the technology of *imagination*, it would be impossible to complete the heavenly assignments we each were sent here to do.

When you use your *imagination to dream* you must set goals for every step of the way. I knew a child who imagined becoming a doctor. They engaged in specific actions along the way that didn't seem like much of anything, but each one was a goal. One of those goals was to go to the library to look through medical journals. Since he wasn't allowed to check them out, he would make a trip to the library just look through medical journals to see what kind of doctor he could become. Once that decision was made, he continued to visit the library to read up on that particular type of doctor. I was amazed at his passion and drive.

This man is now a doctor, caring for people through his own medical practice. His goal of going to the library kept feeding his childhood dream. The goal shifted from looking through medical journals out of curiosity to learning and studying. He had a true commitment to the process of fulfilling his dream. He set goals along the way, and achieved them little by little.

There is a saying, "we don't plan to fail…we fail to plan." I am convinced

> "Life is 10% what happens to you and 90% what you do about it."
> ~Charles R. Swindoll

your success or downfall in life is contained within your *imagination*.

Thomas Edison imagined light; and brought it into the natural realm by creating a light bulb. He had 1,000 failures before the light bulb was invented. Can you *imagine* how many goals he had to put in place each time he walked into his lab.

Imagination helps to manifest the destiny you are carrying in life. You might ask, "does my *imagination* help to define my path, or does my path help to guide my *imagination*?" Well, they actually go hand in hand. Since your *imagination* is built into your DNA, it's the thing God placed inside of you to guide you into your destiny. The things that spark your *imagination* are in line with your designated path. Once you are on your path, your ability to *imagine* new things will be in over drive.

If you are feeling a little lost, here are some questions you can ask yourself to begin to activate your *imagination* to get on the right track.

- What do I REALLY enjoy doing?
- What benefits do people, myself included, gain from the thing I enjoy doing?
- What do others compliment me on the most?
- When I'm envisioning the future…what does it look like for me? What am I doing? Who is around me? What do I see?

Most of us are where we are today because of what we have thought in the recesses of our mind. We make decisions based on what we think. As Henry Ford put it, "Whether you think you can, or you can't, you're right."

We can't blame others for where we are today. If you don't like where you are, what you are doing, and the relationships you are entertaining, you need to look no farther than the mirror. God gave you a great mind. It's up to you how you choose to use it. With His help, and following His path, you will go far. Where there is no vision, there is no goal and therefore; no life.

> *"Whether you think you can, or you can't, you're right."*
> ~ Henry Ford

Now It's Your Turn

There are some who think imagination is not important. However, God speaks to the power of imagination in the story of the Tower of Babel in Genesis 11:1-9. The people were unified and planning to build a tower for their own purposes and fame. Because their pursuits were self-serving, God said, "Let Us go down because they will be able to do whatever they have imagined." If God knew they could do whatever they imagined, He knows you can do whatever you *imagine*, too!

Imagination helps you see into areas you have not able to see before. You have to see in order to understand the potential that has been placed in you.

Remember these keys to using your imagination:
- Your mind can dream and *imagine* beyond your current reality.
- God has given you this powerful technology. Ask Him for revelation on using it.
- Whatever thoughts you fuel will grow. It is vital to think on things that are good and positive.
- Using your imagination to co-create with God is a continual process.
- Not everyone will choose to see what you see or believe what you believe.
- Your words carry power. They will create what you speak.

A great way to get started is to make a pack with yourself to renew your mind daily with fresh imaginations that will cause you to speak positively and develop possibilities all around you.

> *Great minds discuss ideas;*
> *average minds discuss events;*
> *small minds discuss people.*
> ~ Eleanor Roosevelt

Personally, I have found when I experience question marks in my life, doubt begins to set in. Using my imagination gives me hope. I believe imagination is a very real tool that has assisted me in my movement forward. I know it will do the same for you.

Out of seeing a better future, a goal begins to develop, and gives me something to reach towards. It causes a stirring in me that previously wasn't there. A burning desire for what I'm imagining begins to take hold of me. The imagery in my mind begins to bring forth positive thoughts. Words like, "Wow! I think this very thing can become real!" begin to reverberate in my mind.

Now I have a substance, a title deed, perceiving as real fact before it is revealed to the natural senses. Then I pray because I have something tangible to pray about. See yourself getting to the other side and experience that thing you imagined and had the faith to believe.

From the moment you wake up in the morning, start dreaming, start imagining, plot out the course of your day. Then…make it happen. There's a scripture in the Bible that talks about writing out your plan. Habakkuk 2:2 says, "Then the Lord answered me and said, 'Write the vision, and engrave it plainly on [clay] tablets so that the one who reads

Imagination: A Mystical Technology

it will run.'" (AMP)

Set your vision in your mind and call forth those things you can't presently see in the natural. Talk to those ideas until you begin to truly believe them. Speak about them coming to pass with confidence. And take the daily steps to build that reality.

Don't allow your circumstances to dictate your future. Remember, whatever is happening now shall pass. It will not last forever. As long as you're still waking up, you have the opportunity to *imagine*. Imagination is not to be relegated to the level of a childhood fantasy. Imagination is part of your framework. Use it. Exercise it. Step into it!

All creation awaits the manifestations inside of you. Speaking about and acting on the revelation from your imagination releases a frequency needed in the world. What we speak over and over…whether within our mind…or the spoken word…eventually become truth to our subconscious mind and causes an effect. When we change our words, we change our outcome; when we change our outcome, it impacts the world.

True desire in the heart is given by God. It's already yours, so don't forget to pray and ask Him for the strategies and steps to bring it to pass.

I hope this book has encouraged you to ponder the power of the technology of imagination. If so, make this declaration. "I will embark on the imagination journey because it can help me manifest the knowledge of who I really am…and why I am here."

Dr. Jimmie Reed
Global Manifestations

Recommended Resources

Videos

Frequency

Amazing Resonance Experiment! - https://youtu.be/wvJAgrUBF4w

SONIC WATER * KYMAT - https://youtu.be/SjhNqRNuAk8

Power of Words

How words affect us... and our cells - https://youtu.be/WGapwV3Kw8Q

Rice Experiment

Dr Masaru Emoto - https://youtu.be/WWkGw-0sFhM

Books

Living with Purpose: Devotions for Discovering Your God-Given Potential by Dr. Myles Munroe

The Fourth Dimension: Discovering a New World of Answered Prayer by Dr. David Yonggi Cho

About the Author

Dr. Jimmie Reed is the Senior Leader for *Global Manifestations*, in Pueblo, CO. Through practical application and demonstration she helps to prepare individuals for the work of the ministry.

Dr. Reed combines dynamic teaching with compassion and wit while seeking to help bring Heaven's direction to the lives of individuals, to churches, and cities. Ordained through Springs Harvest Fellowship, by Apostle Dutch Sheets, Potential Reed is recognized among ministry leaders as a prophet called to the body of Christ. In addition, Dr. Reed is ordained as a Christian International Prophet by Bishop Bill Hamon of Christian International Network of Churches.

De-mystifying prophetic ministry is a prime focus of her teaching. Called by God to equip believers, she imparts revelation from the Bible to help others become more acquainted with God's voice. "We are able to help each other enter into a deeper walk of intimacy and victory when we allow the Holy Spirit to minister His life through us," says Dr. Reed.

Dr. Reed has a schedule that incorporates leading seminars, conferences, retreats, church services, and prophetic classes where she equips, trains, and activates the saints in apostolic and prophetic ministry. Jimmie carries an anointing for 'BREAKTHROUGH' in many different areas of the lives of those whom she imparts and has begun to move out in signs, wonders, and miracles.

One Last Thing...

If this book has encouraged, challenged, or inspired you, please take a moment to write a review. Please visit any **online bookseller** or **GoodReads.com**, search for this book and leave a review. It would also be an honor if you share this resource on any of your social media pages.

Your review does make a difference in helping others find this resource.

Help us spread the word! Please take a pic of you and your book and post it to social media, tag Dr. Reed by using @GlobalManifestations on both Facebook and Instagram.

Connect with Dr. Reed

Dr. Reed offers mentorship programs, on-demand courses, books, and conferences. Connect with her at Global Manifestations to stay connected and receive notification for all of her training opportunities.

 www.GlobalManifestations.org

@GlobalManifestations

@GlobalManifestations

www.GlobalManifestations.org/YouTube

Dr. Reed's Previous Books

Becoming An Extraordinary Leader: Impacting Others to Lead

Let Me In

Now Is My Time

Weathering Transition: Allowing God to Change You and the Church

Who Me, Prophesy?

Who Me, Prophesy? Journal

Dr. Reed has contributed chapters in the following anthologies:

Destiny: The Other Side of Through

God Met Me Here: Stories of How God Shows up in Everyday Life

www.ingramcontent.com/pod-product-compliance
Lightning Source LLC
Chambersburg PA
CBHW070340120526
44590CB00017B/2967